More Farewells

dear Katy,
wishing you good health
and happiness
in 2022
with love
Amelia

The gift I didn't get to hand to you!

Amelia Fielden

More Farewells

More Farewells
ISBN 978 1 76109 231 2
Copyright © text Amelia Fielden 2021
Cover image: pulpitis from iStock

First published 2021 by
GINNINDERRA PRESS
PO Box 3461 Port Adelaide 5015
www.ginninderrapress.com.au

Contents

Tanka Tales

I want to weep
but the sky has stolen
most of my tears –
rain drenches the last flowers
on his jacaranda

This book is dedicated to dear 'pling,
11 October 1955–27 November 2018
We will always miss you

About the Title

In calling this collection *More Farewells*, I had two things in mind, one serious, one flippant.

Firstly, the title refers to my sadness at having to farewell from this life, over the last few years, a number of family members and friends who were very dear to me. Amongst them, my daughter Kathleen's beloved partner, 'pling Prideaux, to whom this book is dedicated; my stepmother, Anita Walters; and a close friend for sixty-three years, Ray Tomlinson.

Secondly, I was thinking of that old Australian saying about our iconic opera diva, 'more farewells than Dame Nellie Melba'. Because, when I published my previous collection, *These Purple Years*, in 2018, I assured enquirers it was my final book. And yet later I found myself putting together a further collection, *More Farewells*, which just might be my last.

Amelia Fielden

Foreword

As a professor at the University of Utah School of Medicine (1981–2008), my job was to help our physician faculty members become better teachers.

In the last phase of my career, I also found much satisfaction working with multidisciplinary teams to find ways in the curriculum to supplement the Science of Medicine with the Arts...literary, performing and visual.

So I thought it might be fun to write my own poetry, and in 2005 I took a workshop that got me started. Then in 2008, the year of my retirement, I took a haiku workshop. In 2011, I made a New Year's resolution to write tanka. To that end, I began the inductive process of deriving principles of tanka, not by taking a workshop, but by reading tanka by accomplished practitioners.

The first journal editor who accepted my tanka was Amelia Fielden. For me, it was Kismet because, indeed, she was one of the poets whose tanka I had been reading and studying. It is said that good poems make good teachers. I had discovered that her tanka were master teachers.

Thus, what an honour to write this foreword. While some authors write their own introduction, allow me to introduce you to Amelia Fielden as the person I have come to know as a friend and, simply put, as a professional tanka poet extraordinaire.

The word professional is not used here as a noun in the sense of how one gains a livelihood, but rather as an adjective to describe widely accepted and recognised excellence. We also could say that for Amelia tanka is a staple of her daily diet and that this collection of her tanka is a feast to which we, the readers, are welcome guests.

What makes this book special is that Amelia is both a miracle worker and a time traveller.

Let's begin with a cherry blossom tree. One of my favourite tanka in this book is…

> cherry blossoms
> more fragile this spring
> without a dog
> walking the park trails
> I turn back halfway

Cherry blossoms are, of course, iconic in Japanese culture. Amelia is a miracle worker because she, herself, can read Japanese tanka literally, and, as a true poet, can render Japanese tanka into readable English poems that retain, as much as possible, the Japanese aesthetic.

Since this book is not a collection of translations, but her own tanka, why is this important? It is relevant because she brings into the English language the elements of Japanese tanka that have endure for over 1,300 years!

In the tanka tradition, Amelia shares the personal in her life, yet offers her human adventure in a universal manner. Her readers will recognise their own lives in the specifics of the life Amelia has shared in her tanka. Also, she respects the tanka tradition of writing lyrical poems. Read out loud her tanka for yourself and/or recite for loved ones and friends so that you (and they) will hear the song-like quality of her verse.

In this collection, we meet Amelia the time traveller in different phases of her life…as a young, independent woman; wife, mother, and grandmother; maker of friends near and far; visitor to Japan and several other countries.

A bonus of *More Farewells* is that, as well as her solo tanka, we have here tanka sequences which convey a narrative or chronological unfolding of a story, and also tanka strings that are sets of tanka, in any order, sharing a theme or a connecting word or phrase. This collection also includes responsive tanka strings, sets in which Amelia and a colleague take turns, prompting each other to add the next tanka.

In addition, Amelia is skilled at combining short prose with tanka, a form some call 'tanka prose', which she prefers to call 'tanka tales'.

I fathom you will find your favourites in all these variations of tanka. Amelia Fielden, miracle worker and time traveller, has given us a book that I anticipate you will pick off your shelf for more than reading.

Neal Whitman, EdD, Professor Emeritus,
University of Utah School of Medicine
Vice President, United Haiku and Tanka Society

Individual Tanka

Published in *Eucalypt*

two small windows
enough dreaming room
in the attic
she can consider the past
as well as the future

~~~~~

for ten years
as the apple tree
grows and grows,
my hopes diminish –
will she never return

~~~~~

a rickety gate
infused with the fragrance
from spring daphne
opens to my other home –
wild geese honk overhead

lakeside picnics
in summer's dying days
longer darkness
fewer dreams of the future…
I am old, I am old

~ ~ ~ ~ ~

a patience
of surfboard riders
wetsuited,
sitting on a too smooth sea –
so many shades of grey

~ ~ ~ ~ ~

a single hearth
in a cold monocrete house
a single child
with warring parents –
the spaniel sighs as she sleeps

Tideline challenge

'hold on baby' –
hand in hand we float
with the tides
until she swims away
into her own ocean

Weather challenge

(Dried-up waterhole)

water, water
nowhere, nowhere to drink…
through toxic air
birds fly over hollowed mud
into a deadly future.

Pets challenge

cherry blossoms
more fragile this spring
without a dog
walking the park trails
I turn back halfway

~ ~ ~ ~ ~

once in a while
I hear him whinnying
in my dreams
Chico the Shetland pony
doesn't die of neglect

Honourable Mentions in the Mt Fuji
Tanka Grand Prize Contest

2019

> why should I
> climb every mountain
> to find my dream –
> in old age I sleep well
> with the sound of the sea

~ ~ ~ ~ ~

2020

> my love for you
> more permanent than mountains
> or this distance
> between us, enforced now
> by pandemic borders

Published by Chen-ou Liu in his
Never-ending Story, with two Chinese translations

shall I sweep
the courtyard again,
will you come
before my summer ends?
the crimson rose still blooms

Published in *Kokako* journal (NZ)

legacy
of a grandpa long deceased,
the model plane
still on the piano top
waiting for lift-off

~ ~ ~ ~ ~

French lavender
growing in Seattle
the grandchildren
I thought I'd never have –
life fades, life brightens

~ ~ ~ ~ ~

coach swaying
in violent winds
the driver
struggles with the steering wheel –
dust blurs our horizon

my husband dies
the dogs he loved die
my grandchildren grow
taller than their parents –
more fallen leaves to sweep

~ ~ ~ ~ ~

a young tradie
sitting outside the vets'
cradles
his dog's dead body –
social distancing

Published in *Cattails* (online journal)

wind chimes
belling autumn freshness
over the porch –
too soon I'll travel
to cherry trees in bloom

~ ~ ~ ~

coastal doves
as night lightens to dawn
another day
to savour, and walk the beach –
thank you, dear surgeons

~ ~ ~ ~

apple blossoms
blown off, scattering
in wild winds
a magnolia tree
clasps its purple flowers

Published in *Skylark* journal (UK)

the haloed glow
from a streetlight
turns night
into a preview of dawn
for these unlikely lovers

~ ~ ~ ~ ~

new draughts
and old dreams, drifting
through rooms
almost emptied now –
who will buy this pre-loved home

Published in The School of Music Poets'
Silver Fugue chapbook (Australia)

at the crossroads
in the gritty city
questioning
why once I loved living here –
wild birds behind my eyes

Published in *All the Way Home: Ageing in Haiku*,
editor Robert Epstein

turned seventy
I see myself possibly
organising
my stamp collection
when I am old

~ ~ ~ ~ ~

my first lover
has Alzheimer's, now
his wife says
he calls her by my name
on the beach of our past

~ ~ ~ ~ ~

the fragrance
from white lilac subtler
than expected –
letting go of the old age
I had imagined for us

when did he start
walking so slowly?
years and years
of fast strides, and now
what's the rush, he complains

~ ~ ~ ~ ~

so much love
dancing the parquet floor
on Sundays
when the jazz band plays
at the seniors' village

Published in *Atlas Poetica* Special Feature: Tanka of
Flowing Tranquillity

all the blues
of bay, mountain, sky,
one more summer
travelling to the island
in the company of seagulls

Published in *Atlas Poetica* Special Feature:
Humorous Tanka

log cabin life
old-fashioned family fun
for a week
swimming   fishing   hiking
with of course Wifi

Published in *red lights*: responses to Saito Mokichi
tanka

red dragonflies
hover at dusk
over the lily pond –
humming in my head
that old Japanese song*

~ ~ ~ ~ ~

sandpipers
strutting swirling dipping
in sunset sea
reflections of scarlet sky –
how colourful my life

~ ~ ~ ~ ~

through dawn's red light
I can hear the birds stirring
and close by
my dog softly breathing…
another day of life here

~ ~ ~ ~ ~

blood-red roses
tortured into her bouquet,
pure white satin
shrouding her slender form –
the sacrificial bride

* the traditional Akatonbo, Red Dragonfly

Published in *Red Moon* Social Issues Anthology 2020

diner sign
limiting each stay
to half an hour
lest the poor linger
over a packet of fries

~ ~ ~ ~ ~

dove trees blossom
in a nation that threatens war
yet again –
all those complacent faces
on Independence Day

Published in *Ribbons* 'Tanka Café'

Ghosts and Ghouls theme

> August evenings
> in Japanese villages
> the tradition
> of telling ghost stories
> to chill body and soul

~ ~ ~ ~ ~

Relationships

> Gran and Pop
> waltzing harmonising
> 'Always'
> in those days of roses
> with sweet-scented hearts

~ ~ ~ ~ ~

Winter Warmth

> fire in our grate
> red velvet curtains drawn,
> a claret toast
> to the long winter nights
> of conversation and love

What Matters

sixteen nights
of the surf sighing
and my grandson
sleeping in the next bed
fifteen, sixteen, nights

Time theme

capricious Time
you concertina player,
why am I
now a senior citizen
with unfulfilled ambitions

Open theme

that small cousin
cowboy to my Indian,
sharing birthdays
now toasts our seventy-seventh
in vintage champagne

Curiosity theme

so many moves
still to investigate
across the board –
not ready for checkmate
at seventy-eight

'father unknown'
on the birth certificate
his sister named
as his mother – so who were
my real great-grandparents

Escape theme

gentle waves wash
over the sea walls
cradling me
as I swim far away
from sorrows and frustrations

History theme

My first visual memory, other than of home and family members, is of a British black and white newsreel film from February 1952, showing the funeral of King George VI. In my mind's eye, I can still see the three queens – Queen Mary, the King's mother, Queen Elizabeth, his widow, and Queen Elizabeth II, his successor – wearing deepest mourning, faces covered with long black veils – leaving St George's Chapel down the broad stone staircase, in triangular formation. Tall, erect, at 85 years of age, Queen Mary led, with the smaller Elizabeths alongside each other two steps behind.

> black-veiled, three queens
> descend the chapel steps
> at Windsor
> their King's coffin lying in state –
> mother, widow, daughter, silent

Years later, this image was conflated in my imagination with Tennyson's lines in his epic poem 'Morte d'Arthur', describing King Arthur's funeral barge.

> *Black-stoled, black-hooded like a dream*
> *Three queens with crowns of gold – and from them rose*
> *A cry that shiver'd to the tingling stars*

Published in Tanka Society of America Anthologies

Of Love and War and the Life in Between, 2018

sunlight on frost
bare branches against azure
these winter days
of simple loveliness,
cancer free for now

A Thousand Voices, 2019

wisteria…
even as his cancer
grows rampant,
I try colouring my mind
with soft purple flowers

Dance Into the World, 2020

you unwrapped me
from a flowered kimono
on our honeymoon
mapping my body
in a foreign country

Self-portrait, 2021

summer days
filled with a long shrilling
of cicadas,
emptied of much-loved voices –
my roses bloom and bloom

Some individual tanka previously published in my various personal collections, selected and cited by Naomi Beth Wakan in her book *The Way of Tanka* (Canada, 2017)

the years pass
yearning to fly free
love holds me still –
yachts moored near the pier
move just a little

~ ~ ~ ~ ~

'mum, don't you
recognise my voice
any more' –
I blame the connection
but the truth is worse

~ ~ ~ ~ ~

seniors' outing –
becoming aware
I've entered
the time zone where death parts
more often than divorce

~ ~ ~ ~ ~

how I wish
my tanka of passion
did not erupt
solely from old memories –
last night's storm is over

~ ~ ~ ~ ~

'too young
to really be in love'
now too old
to stay awake all night –
where did the between go?

~ ~ ~ ~ ~

hilly paths
I walk where
once I ran –
sometimes the past
must be enough

~ ~ ~ ~ ~

ripeness is all...
perhaps so for peaches, but
ah! those green years
experimenting
careless of time's steady tread

~ ~ ~ ~ ~

we meet again
after fifty-two years...
my teen lover
you were so much taller
in my mind's eye

~ ~ ~ ~ ~

Russian ballet
the elaborate sets
the great leaps...
now to catch the bus home
to 'what's for dinner'

~ ~ ~ ~ ~

two careers
three dogs, five children
those were the days
when the clock panted
to keep up with us

Published in *Under the Basho*, online journal (USA) edited by Jenny Angyal

wheelchair paused
beside the white clematis
he breathes spring
in this lavender air
a flutter of doves

~~~~~

this is home
full of family photos
this is home
where a white dog lives
with our memories

~~~~~

through misty drizzle
a pigeon co-cooing
co-cooing –
no clear idea now
of the best path to take

Unpublished tanka written to prompts at the
Majura Poets' Writing Group, Canberra, Australia

head

soft curly hair
covering a small head
under my hand –
first hard lesson I learned,
the lifespan of a dog

~ ~ ~ ~ ~

home is where
the heart is, so they say –
my old head
misses many homes
and those who lived there

~ ~ ~ ~ ~

headline
on today's front page
all's well –
I'm woken by screaming
       from ambulance sirens

~ ~ ~ ~ ~

touch

> in that culture
> a touch on the shoulder
> interpreted
> as intimacy –
> her headscarf pinned tight

~ ~ ~ ~

connect

> at this time
> we cannot connect your call –
> oh, please,
> I need a voice, not
> a robot…goodbye

~ ~ ~ ~

wave

> think I can see
> my cousin bodysurfing
> a Bondi wave –
> I'm happy looking back
> afraid to look forward

~ ~ ~ ~

treat

this August
tricked by Covid-19
no treat,
no summer overseas
spent with my grandchildren

~ ~ ~ ~

music

the lake's music
is muted, this morning
ripples stilled
birds asleep in the mist –
too noisy, my sad thoughts

~ ~ ~ ~ ~

distance

feeling close
to faraway family
estranged
from an old schoolmate –
distant not always remote

~ ~ ~ ~ ~

draw

I draw a line
through dull yesterday –
with sunshine
and your morning email
I'm more optimistic

~ ~ ~ ~ ~

hope

igniting hope
rose-flames along garden walls –
am I too old
to believe this thing will pass
in my lifetime

~ ~ ~ ~ ~

shift

shifting gears
in her old Toyota
my daughter
backs down the driveway,
ready to leave home

~ ~ ~ ~ ~

bridge

removed now
the flying bridges between
two families
across the Pacific
yearning and facetiming

~ ~ ~ ~

rock

when the Rock
was not called Uluru
our marriage
seemed as solid, but
time crumbled tolerance

~ ~ ~ ~

sink

sinking swimming
sinking swimming all year
how many times
will I survive these waves
of world misfortunes

~ ~ ~ ~

sink

> crossing the world
> for love, seasons reversed
> I reset my clock
> step back into the time
> of teaching kids to swim

~ ~ ~ ~

mask

> unmasked despair
> 'aren't you going to take me?'
> unmasked delight
> 'you're home, it's dinner time' –
> life with a labradoodle

~ ~ ~ ~

spring

> pink and white
> crab apple blossoms
> festoon the trees –
> an old man's face
> opens to the coming summer

Tanka Sequences & Strings

Train Sketches

to Sydney
with high school sports teams
and debaters –
between carriages a friend
stumbles, breaking her leg

falling asleep
in the slow midnight train
through Kyushu,
waking to find next to me
a note *goodbye gaijin girl*

honeymoon trip
on the brand-new bullet train
to Kyoto:
smoother than our marriage,
though shorter in duration

poetry train
grinding past drought landscapes…
on one side
the optimism
of gold wattles

transitioning
from winter to spring
weeping willows
along the water courses…
finally some rain in sight

shorn sheep
scampering away
from the screech
of the train, its jolt
and sway, near Moss Vale

two brown cows
stand in a shallow dam
back to back
how long has it been since
we faced forward together

kangaroos
bounding across paddocks
of dull grass –
our travel from home
not always for love

published in *Poetry in Motion*, Australia

What Lies Within

bus halfway
then the slow shale scrambling
to a hut
just below the summit
of sacred Fuji-san

in cold darkness
waiting with patient crowds
for sunrise –
perhaps this mountain's gods
will reveal themselves today

remnant of snow
around the gaping crater –
slipping, slipping
back down the narrow paths
to Sunday's realities

foreign pilgrim
climbing every mountain,
elusive dreams
long pursued with cameras
and my weary guidebook

published in *Poetry on the Menu*, Australia

Denial

through mall clamour
carol singers persisting
with false cheer –
mid mountain fires, koalas
screaming in their eucalypts

outflying the flames
great clouds of cockatoos
drop from skies
blackened with swirling ash…
sirens sound too far away

young kangaroo
beside a burnt-out forest
no mob
no grass, no water –
the next disaster victim

there are no words
there are no numbers
to express what
we have lost through denial
and our ignorant actions.

published in *Scorched Corners*, Australia

Oregon Holiday, August 2018

A tanka diary Japanese style

3 August

start of trip; drove from Seattle to Canon Beach in Oregon; about four hours. At night, windows wide open to the waves.

> why should I
> climb every mountain
> to find my dream
> in old age I sleep well
> with the sounds of the sea

6 August

at Cape Kuanda; heavy sea mist, steely sea, cool temperatures.. Long walk along the flat wet sand, then waded waist deep into the cold Pacific.

> back and forth
> back and forth, three black dogs
> race for balls
> along the tideline…
> living in the moment

7 August

foggy again in the morning, afternoon sunny and warm. Short drive to a tiny village called Pacific City. Family hired kayaks and paddled for two hours on the river, while I sat on the bank reading.

> silent river
> beneath a cliff of pines
> yellow kayaks
> skimming past blue herons –
> gone, never forgotten

8 August

another grey morning. Checked out of Headlands Hotel and drove to stables. The Seattle four went for an hour's guided beach and dune ride. I found a quaint café nearby where I had a hot Vietnamese coffee.

> riding high
> on his horse, Phantom,
> my grandson
> disappears into sea mist...
> pounding surf on the shore

Drove on to Yachatz vis amazing ice creams at Tillamook.

9 August

took coastal road along cliffs to Seven Mile Beach. Spectacular views. Left Yachatz at noon. Scenic coastal drive to Florence. Ate our sandwiches at the harbor entrance.

> mournful hooting
> from a foghorn that guides
> dory boats
> through the white-outed harbor –
> hide and seek in the dunes

10 August
family ran the beach, and I walked enjoying the dogs and bird life.

> sandpipers
> strutting swirling dipping
> by the grey sea
> a black and white photo…
> fifty years of colour film

11 August
at Cottage Grove resort inland; finally very warm and sunny; blissfully had the outdoor pool to myself all morning while family did tough cycling tour.

> the cool silk
> of a blue pool, rippling
> around me
> worries and the weight
> of many years…banished

12 August
long drive back to Seattle via a stop at the Sunday markets in the small town Vancouver WA.

> summer flowers
> perfuming the warm air,
> kids slurping
> icy poles - how can it be
> winter in my homeland?

published in *The Moorings* Australia

Just in Case

I continue
to coffee-spoon my life
circumspectly
keeping closed for now
its pandora's box

three roses
from a single stem – I
could compare them
to my children, though
one never bloomed

I will keep
all the dogs' collars
just in case
there is a heaven
where we can live together

four years after
his diagnosis
of dementia
come birthday cards inscribed
Many Happy Returns

our old campus
with frog sounds from the creek,
and high above
stars blazing like those nights
we couldn't stop kissing.

published in *International Tanka*, Japan

Movement

across the world
in a long ago life
my small daughter
riding a docile donkey
along the sands at Blackpool

a flock of geese
on the soccer field
kids practise
running and kicking round them –
feathers ruffle in the breeze

skateboarding
past me, a teenager
says to his mate
'Shakespeare classics'
what could be the context?

I used to wear
pretty shoes with high heels
once upon a time
able to dance all night…
need comfy sneakers now

to and fro
on Sydney harbour ferries
to and fro
on flights to America
always travelling for love

published in *International Tanka*, Japan

No Words

between white clouds
a wide blue ribbon sash
at autumn's start
sparrows cluster with fluffed wings
on black overhead wires

seen from above
a slow-moving slide show,
the curve of beach
leash-free for dogs and kids
frolicking in sand and sea

from horizon
to shore, the smooth rolling
of the surf
this mild sunny morning
my cell phone stays silent

we meet
on the grassy headland
hugging, hugging…
no words to console
her devastating news

mindlessness
sweeps over me in waves
higher still
than the ocean pool's walls…
swimming, always swimming

published in *International Tanka*, Japan

Look at the birds of the air...*

vermillion breast
in a camouflage of leaves
king parrot
high on an ash tree...
unfastening my window

speckled wattle birds
framed by crimson-petalled
camellias...
my mother always made me
look pretty, for school dances

rose pink, grey-cloaked
galahs hang upside down
from the swings
in the childless playground...
nearby teenagers texting

unconcerned
at my dog's approach
glossy magpies
striding the dew, tuning up
bright eyes meet bright eyes

in wild grass
two Eastern rosellas
foraging...
so long since his death
I've been blind to beauty

* Matthew 6:26-34
published in *International Tanka*, Japan

Pineapple Daze

pearly dawn…
the hotel yoga teacher
five floors below
wakes me with her commands –
I stretch, turn over in bed

the rainbow ends
in a hibiscus hedge –
this avenue
bloated with mansions
of the hyper rich

a green turtle
in the sea beneath me
swims away
from our encounter…
once in a lifetime

papaya
guava and mango splashed
panorama
tropical sun setting
beyond surfboard riders

at twilight
white pigeons circling
waiting
to roost when the courtyard
clears of other diners

luxury resort:
expecting a tip
my waiter
removes the crumbs
I had left for the birds

Mai Tai night…
banyan trees lighted purple
round the bar
Hawaiian lullabies
crooned to a ukulele

published in *International Tanka*, Japan

Sweet and Sour

Friday nights
in Sydney's Chinatown
a restaurant
above a strange-smelling shop
cluttered with foreign stuff

no tablecloth
on the round laminex
course after course
of savoury dishes
steaming, glistening…yum

boiled white rice
in hand-sized china bowls
with chopsticks
I used more easily
than knife fork and spoon

jasmine tea
from willow-patterned cups
without handles
without milk or sugar –
different manners here

an only child
on those fragrant evenings,
a lucky child
in the post-war forties
of my loved family world

published in *International Tanka*, Japan

Stuck

Monday again
a dew-sparkling morning
magpies carolling –
hard to hear the message
that all's wrong with our world

two o'clock
the day's advancing, while
I'm stuck at home…
another hour to wait
until The Chase, UK

don't touch me
I am vulnerable
to the virus –
yet without your touch
I just feel my age

'stay indoors'
I'm bidden, 'covid-19
could get you' –
the family wants me
to continue cocooning

thinking once more
of my teenage grandchildren,
I watch parrots
through an autumn window…
watch and wait, watch and wait

published in *International Tanka*, Japan

Winter Solstice Walk

this frosty day
three white cockatoos
rasp protests
from a leaf-bare tree...
walking in my down coat

cricketing
on the rough sports field
local kids
stop playing when they see
a puppy bowling over

the lake's music
is muted, this morning
ripples stilled
ducks asleep in the reeds –
too noisy, my worries

sinking swimming
sinking swimming all year
how often
will I ride these waves
of global disasters

the shortest day
of long, patient, months –
winter wattle
flowering bright yellow
in my neighbour's front yard

published in *International Tanka*, Japan

An Incidental Bouquet

between springs
here and overseas
I forget
the intense yellow
of Australian wattle

Dutch iris
a Van Gogh on my wall,
a garden
fill with blue and purple
memories of Tokyo

pink on pink
peach flowers open then fall –
I'm invited
to the spring funeral
of another old friend

streetlights shine
on raindrops slipping
through hedges
starred with azaleas –
Japan in early May

published in *Kokako*, NZ

Easter Sunday At Marino Rocks

a Monet scene
in the Marino garden
autumn poplars
frame small white sailboats
bobbing on daubs of blue sea

date palm arms
beckon rainbow lorikeets
Barbary doves
walk on iron balustrades
breakfasting with the birds

back and forth
back and forth, pigeons calling
recalling
coastal childhood years
cousins and grandparents

published in *Kokako*, NZ

Patient

hospital nights
bright light, hard narrow bed,
staff chattering…
desperation sleep
finally closes me down

even before
the pale light of dawn
they come
with medications
and blood pressure machines

at my age
fancy wanting my mother,
but who else
could make it all better –
breakfast trolley approaching

in a nightgown
of fiery blue, I question
nurses
as young as my grandchildren –
what do they know

tree patterns
against an uncertain sky
clouds clustering –
how much longer must I
worry and wonder

published in *Kokako*, NZ

Not a Grandchild, But

with wordless
warm companionship,
the rescue dog
saves my long days
from their emptiness

this presence
in my widowed life
exceeds his size –
together we explore
city parks and sea shores

learning the beach
the golden dog ventures
into the surf,
digs through soft sand,
not a grandchild, but…

my dog lies dying
cold rain falls, all day long
what can I do
but wait for this to end –
the white rose drops its petals

all that remains
on a windless blue day
his ashes
settle into the earth
under my eucalypt tree

six o'clock
awakened by the ghost
of a small dog
begging for breakfast –
his bowl stays empty

published in *Skylark*, UK

Norfolk Island Sojourn

A travel diary Japanese style

welcomed
by yellow hibiscus
in smiling bloom
I exit the airport
to paradise island

this swimming pool
is a sky-blue sheet
rumpling
under my breaststroke –
three bantams cross the lawn

palm fronds
outside my window
flick sun patches
onto the gauze curtains –
such random patterns

greying retriever
living out his tired life
at the resort
greets my friendly words
with blind indifference

as we wait
on a western clifftop,
sunset comes
the sea turns silver, then gold –
some days are diamonds

the last clouds
and colours of the day
framing
an indigo ocean –
two bright stars appear

between lush hedges
of an island lane,
four plump cows
and a bus full of women
eyeballing each other

pawpaws
hang from palm trunks, swaying
against azure
a bulging black heifer
looks ready to calve

Emily Bay:
turquoise waters, protected
by coral reefs
and dense strands of pines –
swimming to lose myself

here and there
through the rain-wet garden
come chirrupings –
tomorrow's schedule
a Bird Discovery tour

captured
and neatly labelled
the wild flora
of Norfolk Island
in a green-fenced park

Norfolk pines
climbing misty hills
poincianas
dripping from outstretched limbs –
no sun splashes today

rainforest walk:
deeper and deeper
into the green
tracing the call
of a gerrygone bird

Ansen Bay spring:
goslings, calves, tourists
walk cliff pastures
above the wild waves
white terns flying in pairs

in Morocco
purple bougainvillea,
on Norfolk
scarlet bougainvillea,
everywhere, thorns

published in *Skylark*, UK

Water, Water Everywhere

woken at six
by the garden sprinklers.
I lie in bed
waiting for the boy to play
Schumann on his piano

while they run
to the swimming centre
I stroll
along lakeside paths, content
to be past competing now

lap after lap
commanded by their coach –
the air is thick
with the smell of chlorine
and Olympic yearnings

'too long
in the shower,' I scold
'water
is not for wasting,
when did it last rain?'

outside the pool
we feel mist and moisture
through the park
the first raindrops trickle
over still-wet blond heads

published in *Skylark*, UK

Not All Roses and Chocolates

Valentine's Day
birthday of my best friend –
wartime baby,
what would her future be
under Japanese rule

'we' won; she grows
and draws scarlet love hearts
on the card
for a rock 'n' roll boy,
dreaming 'love me tender'

white wedding
to honour and obey
young bridegroom
as nervous as she
on their island honeymoon

they multiply:
one daughter, two grandsons
working, playing
happy families
in a seaside city

'two to five months'
collapses the house of cards –
her funeral
on November fourteenth
palely pink with gerberas

published in *Atlas Poetica*, US

Time Passes

the driftwood
we left on the beach
the dreams
we dared to confide…
to whom do they belong now

engagement photo
at Lake Yamanaka
the mountain
rising snow-streaked behind,
in the foreground just us

my mother said
'this one's a keeper' –
she was wrong
he drifted away
into an early death

shifting
from foot to foot
edging
out of the doorway
my stepson leaves home

bare limbs
now clad in green leaves –
I glance away
and my children move on
into their distant lives

published in *Atlas Poetica*, US

Inside the Bamboo Gate

tranquillity
boundaried by the roar
of traffic –
a gold koi gulps
between waterlily pads

summer sky
clear of all but flashes
from silver jets…
carefully placing my feet
on the cobblestone paths

stepping stones
expand the distance
across a stream
three small turtles
crowd one small rock

reflected
in the cloudy green pond
at the heart
of this Japanese garden,
her bright turquoise sweater

shimmering blue
a butterfly brushes
the stone deer
on the Kasuga lantern –
somewhere a waterfall

children at play
outside the bamboo gate
flying kites,
riding bikes, unrestricted
by Japanese aesthetics

published in *red lights*, USA

Notes From a Summer Visit to Seattle

the cool silks
of Green Lake rippling
around me...
buoyant again I banish
the weight of many years

ripening
too fast, purple plums
fall from their tree –
already she's writing
essays for college entrance

white sails scudding
over deep blue water,
white wings dipping
in the soft salt breeze
ferry ride through Puget Sound

Harbour seals
flipping through their fiord
of azure,
a sea plane rises into
the span of summer sky

turquoise-winged
dragonflies drifting
on a leaf boat
across the lake's dark water
always shadows behind light

published in *red lights*, USA

Last Stop Before Canada

warm lit empty
the waiting rooms waits
while I wait
in the drizzly darkness
for an errant Yellow Cab

curtains open
on a steel blue morning
pavement puddles
disappear along the way
to downtown Bellingham

red brick and tile
turreted fantasy,
this museum
of dead marine exhibits
and lively poets

from train tracks
to wide sunset horizon,
rippling sea
the focus of my thoughts –
suddenly a tunnel

published in *red lights*, USA

One Misstep

stranded
between night and day
in the heat
of a summer bedroom
she pictures waterfalls

waterfalls
all round the rock walls
in the valley
a nervous hiker
stranded on the steep edge

the steep edge
of her frail eighties –
one misstep
and she'll be stranded
in a nursing home

a nursing home
corridor of wheelchairs
entangled
with nightmares and dreams
stranded...

published in *red lights*, USA

Sydney, December 2019–January 2020

jingle bells
louder and longer
sirens
speeding to the flames
this season of bushfires

kookaburras
in conversation
crack the dawn –
at Coogee Beach now
a chattering grandma

streaked with silver
by the sun between clouds,
the sea unrolls –
back to the beginning
I swim, young again

twenty twenty:
on shiny red light rail
I am missing
my fifties' family,
not those old green rattlers

swift clouds of gulls
above a platinum ocean –
inland wild life
scattering through the fires
dying in toxic air

published in *red lights*, USA

Wishing

my flights this year
in the magic Wishing Chair*
take me to where
I have been before, yet
may never go again

family living
in the west of my country,
and in the west
of American chaos –
they stay there, I stay here

love being beamed
electronically now,
only hope
flies over sea and land
in my magic Wishing Chair

* *The Adventures of the Wishing Chair*, Enid Blyton, 1937
published in *red lights*, USA

That Summer

lunching
on the sunlit terrace
with an old friend
talking about a 'good death'
as something quite remote

silver birches
forming a leafy frieze
by the river
a father and son fish –
this final holiday month

twilight dappling
an elk in the meadow
with his herd –
will anyone care
to read my diaries

wind music
high in the spruce trees
low on the lake…
first notes of a Mozart
clarinet concerto

published in *Ribbons*, USA

A Season of Mellow Fruitfulness in Nara

persimmons
chestnut parfaits, fried oysters
November
menus to invigorate
jaded summer appetites

at Kasuga
climbing the hilly curves
cool stone lanterns
and perspiring tourists –
deer step lithely through the grass

old noodle house
by an even older pond...
I focus on
a five-storeyed pagoda,
ignore the passing cars

cast in bronze
young girl playing her flute
all day long
outside the Craft Museum
volunteer guides in yellow

so many shades
of autumn in the maples
overhanging
steep stairs to the temple...
praying for lung power

John Keats, 'Ode to Autumn', 'Season of mist and mellow fruitfulness'
published in *Ribbons*, USA

Too Many Hours

single again
in a double room
so much space
in which to miss you –
piling pillows on my bed

apricot dawn
spreading across the sky
the sun rises
from beyond the silver sea –
where have all the stars gone

if I can live
today without you, then
I can manage
tomorrow, maybe…
doves are cooing somewhere

daily plunge
into an ocean pool
letting the waves
overwhelm my sadness –
on the rocks, tiny crabs

too many hours
until dark night's dreaming,
too many hours
I'm alive and you are not
…except in my spirit

published in *Ribbons*, USA

Long-distance Love

sixteen nights
of the surf sighing
and my grandson
sleeping in the next bed...
sixteen summer nights

no rain for weeks...
now Eastern rosellas
fluttering
in puddles on the path,
bright brollies at the bus stop

growling
round my house, the west wind
grows fiercer –
another winter
of long-distance love

apple blossom
blown off, scattering
who knows where –
the magnolia tree
clasps its crimson flowers

guardian
of my grandchildren
Mt Rainier
soars snow-topped below
my flight from far away

published in *Ribbons*, USA

Igniting Hope

this winter
tricked by covid-19
no treat,
no summer overseas
with my grandchildren

at eleven
rain eases, we go walking
a small white dog
with a woman wearing red,
just the two of us

twenty-four
pink-breasted galahs
foraging
on the field, oblivious
to social distancing

sunny courtyard
a basket of washing
to hang out,
when did this become
an event, not a chore

igniting hope
rose-flames along garden walls –
am I too old
to believe this thing will pass
in my lifetime

published in *Ribbons*, USA

Elegies: Some Tanka Reflections

my slow days
in gas fired warmth
looking out
at grey winds sweeping
the remnants of autumn

finally
on the elm young leaves
fluttering
the morning after
my friend's last breath

spring sunlight
on four dear faces
by a cherry tree
frothed with pink flowers –
all gone now, every one

Gran and Pop
waltzing, harmonising
'Always'
in those days of roses
with sweet-scented hearts

all that remains
on a windless blue day
his ashes
settle into the hole
under our eucalypt

published in *Stacking Stones, An Anthology of Short Tanka Sequences*

Untested Depths

not quite light
outside the first birds chirp
and close by
my dog's soft breathing…
another day of life

a parrot thuds
against my kitchen window –
dark despair
in the prime minister's voice
on TV's *Today Show*

morning fog
deeper and deeper into
isolation –
first buds on the prunus,
*if winter's come**

so high, the price
for staying safe and well…
I wave
to neighbourhood children,
withholding my hugs for now

unchanging
this widow's lakeside walk –
smooth waters
reflect my resolution
to keep on living

* 'if winter's come, can spring be far behind': 'Ode to the west wind',
by Percy Bysshe Shelley
published in *Stacking Stones, An Anthology of Short Tanka Sequences*

More Meanderings

Another September: the wattles' bright yellow beside the paths is repeated in constellations of wild daisies through the park

daisy chains
fragile gifts exchanged
in friendships
which have held for sixty years –
so many funerals now

cautiously
walking from covid winter
into spring,
I glimpse deep purple iris
through a half-open gate

over a fence
branches of scarlet blossom
dark as blood plums –
is this year headed towards
summer bushfires again

outside the café
tulips flame in a cage
to save them
from marauding possums –
nature versus nurture

published in *Stacking Stones, An Anthology of Short Tanka Sequences*

Tanka Tales

Back Then

many things
forgotten in old age,
still able
to list the names and dates
of all the dogs I've loved

When I was very young, Mum, Dad, Biddy the cocker spaniel and I lived in Powell Street. From a child's point of view the best thing about this street was the lane behind the houses. Each backyard had a gate opening into the lane. Rubbish bins went out there, and were emptied daily into a truck manned by garbos in blue singlets. Bread and milk were delivered by horse-drawn carts. The baker sold loaves of white bread 'wrapped' in slips of paper. Housewives…and there was one in every home…took aluminium billies out to the milko to be filled from giant vats. The milk was then kept in our kitchen ice chest, for which a block of ice was carried from another cart in the lane by a huge man with a sack on his back.

Like the iceman, others traded along the lane once a week or so: the rag and bone man who bought old cloth, the rabbito, who sold skinned rabbits for the pot, and the clothes prop man. Mum didn't cook rabbit, but now and again we needed a new clothes prop. After being boiled in the laundry copper, washing was hung on lines strung between gum tree branches with splits cut in their tops.

Our fences were timber palings. Up them straggled choko vines and sweet peas in the backyards, and honeysuckle and morning glory in the lane. Blackberries grew sweet and free for the picking.

Mum's out the back
with her billycan
and I'm skipping
down honeysuckle lane
under morning glory sky

published in *International Tanka*, Japan

Watching the Waves

Even then they must have been dear. We never had cherries in the rented suburban cottage where I lived with mum and dad. Only at my grandparents' place, and only once a year, at Christmas.

We feasted on roast turkey and ham, followed by slabs of traditional pudding with threepenny bits in it. Then dishes of nuts, glacé fruits, mixed lollies, and a big cut-glass bowl of black cherries appeared. No one was hungry by then...

On Boxing Day we relaxed. One year, I remember, most of the family went off to South Head, to watch the start of the annual Sydney to Hobart yacht race. Grandma and I chose to stay at home.

For lunch we had Christmas leftovers. Overlooking Coogee Beach, in the small dining room that doubled as my holiday bedroom, we sat and sat, talked and nibbled, talked and nibbled.

> *together*
> *my grandmother and I*
> *emptying*
> *her favourite bowl*
> *of her favourite fruit*

published in *Haibun Today*, online

The Geometry Lesson

I was 16. He was 20. She was 34.
I was a schoolgirl. Pretty. Unsophisticated.
He was the Sword of Honour officer cadet at the Military Academy.
She was a woman of the world, beautiful and charming.

He was my boyfriend, but she was my mother

At dawn after the Graduation Ball I offered him my virginity
He declined affectionately, honourably, explaining, 'I don't love you.'

Much later I understood what he had meant was, 'I don't love *you*.'

We lost our handsome captain at the battle of Long Tan.

> *only I am left*
> *to remember now*
> *that true romance*
> *from the last century –*
> *violets are not blue**

---

* 'Roses are red, violets are blue, the honey is sweet and so are you' is
a classic children's rhyme.

published in *Ribbons*, USA

Beyond the Rainbow

From the time I was very young. I have loved learning and naming shades of colour.

> *wild parrots,*
> *dahlias in our garden,*
> *my father*
> *could tell me all their colours*
> *and answer all my questions*

My best ever birthday present was a set of one hundred Derwent coloured pencils, stamped with names I roll around on my tongue: heliotrope, mauve, lilac, lavender, violet, purple…

Many years later my mother lay dying, drifting in and out of consciousness. The children and I visited her every day in hospital. We would tell her what was happening, hoping she could hear us and know we were still including her.

The day before Grandma stopped breathing, Kathleen moved closer to the bed, lifted her T-shirt and said, 'We're going to swimming in the river. Look, I just got a new swimsuit. Don't know what colour to call it.'

Opening her eyes for the last time, my mother gazed at Kathleen's tummy and pronounced in a clear voice *cinnamon*.

> *no need*
> *to say 'I love you',*
> *no need*
> *to say 'I've been happy…'*
> *cinnamon suffices*

published in *Kokako*, NZ

The Last Time I Saw Paris

A bone-chilling winter. Low-hanging icicles have closed the Eiffel Tower to tourists. Snow has fallen again overnight. On the long hill, steep steps to the gleaming dome of Sainte Chapelle are crusted with ice, as we make our ascent from Monmartre metro station.

The Place des Arts is deserted save for a lone painter in an army great coat. Shivering, I glance at his canvas, a skeleton tree shrouded under a blur of impressionistic grey clouds.

Around the corner, in a twisting lane, we find a small bistro beaming light onto the cobbles. Inside, an old-fashioned wood stove crackles with heat.

>   *oak table*
>   *by the window, curtained*
>   *in red velvet,*
>   *two glasses of burgundy*
>   *reflecting candle flames*

Beyond the window, snowflakes swirl from the darkening sky. Neon lights flicker the name *Le Lapin Qui Rit*.* above the entrance to a hole-in-the-wall bar across the way.

>   *the rabbit laughs*
>   *as my lover lies to me*
>   *ah, Paris,*
>   *City of Light, what passions*
>   *have smouldered, then died here*

* The Laughing Rabbit
published in *The Moorings*, Australia

Two Students, One Sky

When I was a new graduate in Japan, I met a young man who proposed under the heavy purple sky of the Eastern Capital*

> *neons flashing*
> *exhaust smoke speeding*
> *through the alley –*
> *'whatever happens*
> *will you marry me?'*

Back home in Australia there followed years of raising a family, teaching Japanese in high school, and – from time to time – hosting exchange students

> *every night*
> *the girl from Tokyo*
> *checks out*
> *our Southern Cross stars*
> *captures them in her diary*

* The name Tokyo means Eastern Capital
published in *Atlas Poetica*, USA

Generations

hot afternoon –
waiting on the corner
a young woman
wearing long black velvet,
mourning or masquerade

When Gran died my mother forbade me take my two daughters to the service.
'It's no place for young children,' she declared, insisting they attend school as usual.

Years afterwards. Catherine and Isabelle criticised me for that. I did not blame their now-deceased grandmother, just letting it be added to the list of my failings as a mother.

Thirty years later, it was taken for granted that my three-year-old granddaughter would attend her aunt's funeral.

retired now
I drive past a school
pondering
decisions that seem right
at the time…

published in *International Tanka*, Japan

Windows

southerlies
riding white horses
through the bay
forever in rhythm
with grandmother's tales

My grandparents lived forty years in a flat on the northern hill above Coogee Beach. I often stayed with them. My bed was in the back room, a room filled with the beach view and sounds of the Tasman Sea. There I slept the deepest of sleeps.

suck and thump
suck and thump, surf
against sand
a Sydney lullaby
sung through salt-smeared windows

As a teacher on exchange in Kyushu, I shared an apartment on the tip of a peninsula dividing Hakata Harbour from the Japan Sea. My housemate chose the Western-style front bedroom, leaving for me the tatami room, with a wall of glass overlooking the water.

ocean liners
glide past bonsai islands
while I sip tea
turning the bowl to admire
its familiar foreign form

Echoes from the water were gentler than at Coogee, but they had the same lulling effect on my nights.

Older now, I've made three visits to friends living on the Canadian island of Gabriola, an island accessible only by ferry.

> *two seagulls*
> *perched on a short plank*
> *facing*
> *in opposite directions*
> *as it drifts through the straits*

The Salish Sea surges onto the pebbly strand below my friend's wild clifftop garden.

> *otters in the mist*
> *among swathes of grey satin*
> *over the bay*
> *ripples widen, dark heads*
> *surfacing, disappearing*

French windows opened wide in the guest room I watch moonlight on the waves, then sleep and wake to their cadence.

> *narrowing*
> *with each high tide*
> *the strand and my life*
> *fade in the twilight*
> *and yet, and yet*

published in *Haibun Today*, online

Assumptions

At the end of my jog around the lake parklands, I sink down on a bench at the Community Centre's wading pool. Nearby is an elderly gentleman, white-haired and white-skinned, relaxing on a folding chair facing the pool. The adjacent bench is occupied by an elderly lady wearing baggy shorts and a T-shirt. In looks she might be his twin, but in manner she seems to be his spouse. Beside her are spread various art supplies. She holds a small canvas and is painting the scene in front of her with concentration.

I assume that the couple has come to this location to enjoy, and in her case to record, the colourful sight of a myriad young children playing in and out of the large expanse of shallow water.

Then, from out of the crowd a very small person approaches the artist. In the politically incorrect olden days of Australia, he or she would have been dubbed a picanniny. On skin the rich tones of mahogany, the only clothing is a bright blue swim nappy. The child's head of tight black curls rests on the lady's pale knees as a little voice mumbles 'wanna cookie'.

> *appalled*
> *that I wanted to study*
> *Japanese,*
> *my uncle said 'I fought*
> *those bastards in the war'*

published in *Haibun Today*, online

Op. 15 No. 1,* Seattle, 5 August 2016

Summer morning. Sunlit green maple leaves crowd into the tall opened windows.

Between them an upright piano. Wearing only superhero underpants and orange socks, a young boy is playing Schumann.

> *'Scenes from Childhood'*
> *overlapping love*
> *for this boy*
> *for this music – unearned,*
> *the richness of my life*

* Composed by Robert Schumann (1810–1856)
published in *Ribbons*, USA

True Measures

His outfit is new: white shirt, black tie and trousers, shiny lace-up shoes. But the focused face as he walks onto the stage, holding his clarinet, is not new to me. I have seen that expression many times – when he mounts a starting block at the pool, when he crosses a finish line at the track, when he sits down at the piano.

> *a long while yet*
> *until he becomes a man –*
> *the conductor*
> *raises her baton,*
> *this is the beginning*

published in *Ribbons*, USA

In the Eye of the Beholder

Pelindaba lavender farm on San Juan island.
Rolling fields of palest purple mist.
A faint perfume on the breeze
'Look, a shop,' spots my young grandson.
'Maybe they have ice cream.'

They do and it's honey-lavender ice cream, made on the farm.
We sit in a garden courtyard, bees busy in the flowering bushes
around us.

'This is beautiful,' sighs his sister, gazing into her tub of sweet
treat. I wonder whether there's an ice cream stand in Monet's
water garden at Giverny. If not, I might hold off the aesthetic
education of these kids for a few more years.

> *relaxing*
> *into this moment…*
> *their childhood*
> *will pass swift as cloud-shadows*
> *over the lavender fields.*

published in *Skylark*, UK

December Park

oh, why did
our mothers encourage us
to marry
older men – those voices
from a wail of windows

They are here again today in Volunteer Park, slowly walking the same path. Just on dusk. She, in her customary cheerful pink parka, white hair uncovered. He, tall and emaciated, clad in shades of charcoal. Her hand clasps his left elbow, steering his shuffling gait. Under a black woollen beanie his head is bowed as he manoeuvres a cane with trembling right hand.

A mandarin duck appears; goes waddling along behind them. Concentrated on safe progress the couple does not seem to be aware of their feathered follower.

Old and practised lovers, these strangers passing in the December park.

reflected
in the reservoir
winter trees
tarnish its silver…
'the sun also sets'

* Reference is to the 1926 novel by Ernest Hemingway, *The Sun Also Rises*

published in *Skylark*, UK

Two Spring Days

During my longish life I have only twice had the delight of visiting a dedicated peony garden. Both gardens are in Japan.

The first time was in 1969. Living then in Tokyo. I learned from a local paper of peonies in full bloom, at a temple north of the city. On a work free day Derek and I caught a train there, with our small daughter in a pushchair. We were overwhelmed by the rainbow spectrum and lushness of the spring flowers. The many slide photographs we took were later lost in our divorce, but I have the mental pictures to this day.

> *April Love*
> *so young, so hopeful*
> *golden yellow*
> *deep crimson, fragile pink*
> *colour prints in my heart*

Almost half a century later, with a dear friend from student days, I discover a second peony paradise. This one lies within the grounds of the Hachimangu Shrine, a popular tourist destination in the historic town of Kamakura, south of Tokyo.

Strolling up the long crowded avenue towards the scarlet shrine, we notice, off to the side of a large lotus pond, bamboo fencing and a gate with a discreet sign, 'Peony Garden'. There are few people inside, and we wander joyfully among the beds of brilliant blooms planted under cherry blossom trees lining the banks of the pond.

> *a chance visit*
> *maybe the last chance*
> *together*
> *we take photos to show*
> *our grandchildren*

published in *Atlas Poetica*, Japan

Monet's Magpie

In the Adelaide Art Gallery, the vibrant paintings of an Impressionist exhibition* are hung in separate galleries according to their dominant colours.

Before being surrounded by blues, greens, purples, and reds, I walk through the 'black room' of somber canvases.

And then into the subdued glory of the 'white room'. One wall is dominated by Monet's masterpiece. *La Pie*.† So many hues of white, lapsing into icy-blue shadows. Some streaks of brown on the stile, walls, and tree trunks. In the background two red chimney dots. My eye is drawn to one tiny black and white bird, almost a blob, in the middle left of this painting.

> *a reject*
> *of nineteenth-century*
> *Paris salons,*
> *now at the Musée d' Orsay*
> *this magpie, the most loved*

---

* *The Colours of Impressionism*, Adelaide, April 2018.

† *La Pie* means 'the magpie'– According to visitor surveys, this painting is currently the most popular of Monet's works in the Musée d' Orsay.

published in *The Moorings*, Australia

Nara Encounter 1: Another Two Cakes

Nara, 14 November 2018

> *though it feels warm*
> *this season is autumn, so*
> *scarlet and gold*
> *plastic leaves proliferate*
> *through the shopping streets*

After wandering the lanes of Nara Old Town, and browsing the traditional stores in covered arcades for hours, I am heading back to my hotel. The aroma of fresh coffee entices me into a smart, Western-style café.

At the counter I purchase a drink and a cake, which I carry on the tray provided to a small table for two between empty tables.

I have almost finished my cake, a mont blanc topped with chestnut puree, when I notice a woman seating herself at the next table diagonally opposite me. The woman looks like my Japanese mirror-image; about the same age and height, with short silver hair in a straight bob cut. We are both wearing grey cashmere sweaters. Her tray contains the same as mine; a medium-size black iced coffee, and a mont blanc cupcake.

Our eyes meet. I say in Japanese, 'This is really delicious. Mont blancs have been my favourites from way back.'

'Mine too,' she responds, smiling at me as she picks up her cake fork. Both too reserved apparently, for further conversation, we concentrate on our respective treats.

In a while, I see that the woman has put on spectacles – with frames just like mine...

and is absorbed in a book. I don my own reading glasses to write in my diary.

> *fancying she*
> *is me in another life,*
> *I record*
> *this once-off meeting...*
> *outside, dusk dims the leaves*

* This reference is to the title of a tanka prose piece 'A Tale of Two Cakes', in my 2012 book *Mint Tea from a Copper Pot & Other Tanka Tales.*
published in *International Tanka*, Japan

Nara Encounter 2: Hers Are White, Mine Are Yellow

a nine-hour flight
lands me in Japanese,
a comfort zone
with a different pattern –
persimmons on leafless trees

As my taxi turns into a narrow street of the Old Town, I notice rows of traditional low wooden houses with racks of drying persimmons outside their windows. Opposite stands the Onjōkan, a large modern edifice of white-painted ferroconcrete, containing galleries and an auditorium where today's Sister City Anniversary tanka concert is to be held.

At the entrance, bowing in welcome, is Mrs. K, who was so hospitable to me when I was performing in Nara five years ago. We have not been in contact since. Over cans of coffee from a convenient vending machine, I ask how she has been.

'Actually, I had a terrible time last year. In April I was diagnosed with breast cancer and had to have my right breast removed. Two months later, I was in a bad car accident. My car was damaged beyond repair, but luckily I survived with only injuries to my shoulder.'

I express my concern, then share with her the story of my own 2017: my husband's death in April, a car accident in May, the removal of my cancerous right breast in June.

We exclaim over these awful coincidences. 'But how are you doing now?' I continue.

'I feel fine. No more treatment except for one small white pill with breakfast everyday.'

'Same here, but my magic pill is yellow.'

'By the way,' she adds, 'I find I'm writing quite a lot of tanka about breast cancer, these days. Are you?'

'Well, not for now. I haven't felt like putting those experiences into poetry. Maybe later.'

Exchanging smiles, without words we acknowledge our similarities and differences.

> *'seize the day'*
> *what else are we to do…*
> *today will go*
> *as scheduled, no guarantees*
> *given for tomorrow*

published in *The Moorings*, Australia

Nara Encounter 3: He Held My Hand

crimson maples
around the lonely lake
white row boats
empty of courting couples –
mid autumn in Yoshino

Far from Nara city, the mountainous region of Yoshino is still within Nara prefecture. This cool blue morning my translation colleague urges me up a long steep slope in the forest to the Yoshimizu Shinto Shrine. Well-acquainted with the shrine's chief priest, she has come to finalise arrangements for a tanka concert to be held there on 5 January, as part of the New Year celebrations

Sipping bowls of deep green tea, the three of us settle on the verandah overlooking a valley of breathtaking autumn colours. Clad in scarlet and gold brocade robes and a lacquered black headdress in the style of 1,300 years ago, the grey-bearded priest is welcoming and talkative. He explains to me that he used to be a police inspector, heading a murder squad in the big smoke of Osaka. At fifty, he quit the force and retrained as a priest to perform year-round religious ceremonies, conduct weddings according to the Shinto rites,* and pray for world peace.

He gives me scroll with his favourite saying 'the world is a family' spelled out in Japanese calligraphy.

It seems that this man of many parts is also a keen poet, as the conversation veers from world peace to tanka writing. Decrying the frequently somber tones, of much contemporary tanka… apparently there is a whole sub-genre of 'suicide tanka' in Japan now…he exhorts us to teach 'happy tanka' in our workshops.

His tanka philosophy is that the seeking out of bright details to express them in poetry is a necessary counterbalance to the dark side of life.

The morning is advancing and with it other visitors to the shrine. Noriko and I now attempt to take our leave. He sees us to the way out. Then to my amazement, the Reverend Sato takes my hand and, holding it firmly in his, guides me down the slope lest I fall. This is a culture in which physical contact with strangers is rare, but he held my hand today.

> *one by one*
> *little golden fans flutter*
> *from gingko trees –*
> *holding onto hope*
> *until the very end*

* In contemporary Japan, weddings are usually Shinto ceremonies while funerals are conducted in temples by Buddhist priests.

published in *Haibun Today*, online

Sweet Thoughts

I have decided that the lamington choc top is the best invention since air conditioning for cars.

On a heatwave afternoon I hand over $5 at the candy bar, reminiscing.

> *teenagers*
> *with fund-raising lamingtons*
> *all over*
> *the kitchen, icing sugar*
> *cocoa, coconut and crumbs*

Ah, those hazy crazy days of trying to be a good mother.

This January, I'm a self-indulgent grandmother luxuriating in a cooled cinema, while slurping on a delicious combination of desiccated coconut, dark chocolate, and vanilla ice cream with raspberry ripple…made by someone else.

> *'do as I say*
> *not as I do' – somehow*
> *they turned out*
> *all right, now it's time*
> *to teach their kids to cook*

published in *Kokako*, NZ

All Right Now?

When I visit my ninety-six-year-old stepmother for perhaps the last time, we do not talk about death. As I stoop to kiss her goodbye, she suddenly says, 'What is love? Your father and I didn't have a smouldering passion, but we were always happy to be together.'

> *birdsong morning*
> *feels so far away –*
> *shifting*
> *anxieties and stiff legs*
> *I embrace my pillow*

> *walking the dog*
> *between foggy sky*
> *and damp paths…*
> *even the magpies*
> *have muted their voices*

> *here comes the sun**
> *but it's not all right now –*
> *eyes clouded*
> *at 'pling's funeral*
> *I try to keep on singing*

* 'Here Comes the Sun' by George Harrison, 1969
published in *Haibun Today*, online

Wild Canaries

I'm travelling on the coach from Sydney International Airport to Canberra. Now in Australia. Still feeling not quite home. Drifting backwards in time.

> *September*
> *yellow wattles all along*
> *the highway*
> *that's speeding my return*
> *from summer in Seattle*

> *between seasons*
> *between continents*
> *I've forgotten*
> *the eye-catching brightness*
> *of wattle trees in full bloom*

Determined not to succumb to jet lag by taking an afternoon nap. I stroll with my dog around our suburban streets and parklands.

> *rebel wattle*
> *wavering, struggling to fly*
> *with spring winds*
> *like a golden cloud*
> *of wild canaries*

published in *Kokako*, NZ

Giant Steps*

As late as 2003, there existed in France ancient legislation banning women from appearing in public clad in trousers.

> *Dominique*
> *sleek-limbed in black leather*
> *stands on the stage*
> *discussing poems and dance…*
> *a pirouette of tutus*

As for me, an audience member, I have not owned a skirt this century.

* International Poetry Studies Institute symposium, 'Small Leaps, Giant Steps', October 2019

published in *The Moorings*, Australia

Purple Thoughts

These days, when I don't always readily recall the exact title of a film seen last week, random encounters can recreate the circumstances of long ago.

Spring again. This afternoon, walking my dog, I pass a cottage with a ramshackle fence draped in luscious wisteria.

> *in plump branches*
> *pale purple and white petals*
> *scent the air*
> *summoning the bees,*
> *restoring memories*

It is not a scene from nature, of which this Canberra wisteria now reminds me, but a Japanese ornament. Fifty years ago, in Tokyo, my elder daughter was given a porcelain doll dressed in geisha dancing costume, and carrying a branch of wisteria in bloom. I've no idea what became of that.

But this evening I have chatted on the phone with my daughter for over an hour.

> *so many moves*
> *too many treasures*
> *discarded*
> *along the way – love*
> *and wisteria enduring*

published in *International Tanka*, Japan

Plenty of Pineapples, But

The music of the Pacific Ocean swells into my hotel room. I sleep and wake to the rhythm of the waves breaking on the shore.

Strolling the dawn beach I see no little bird imprints in the wet sand. Missing, too, is that characteristic screeching. Where are the sea gulls?

Are there no seagulls here, I ask a surfboard attendant?
No, ma'am, he confirms, no seagulls.
Seagulls abound in Sydney and Seattle. Why not in Waikiki?

Puzzled, I later consult the internet and find this information:

…'the habitat of the Hawaiian Islands is not right for them. Gulls are primarily scavengers so they are often found along continental coasts and shallow inland waters where there is sufficient food.'

Well, well – a beach holiday without seagulls!

> *through palm trees*
> *a flight of white pigeons –*
> *fish and chips*
> *without eyeballing*
> *by feathered predators*

published in *The Moorings*, Australia

Sweet Songs of Youth Were Sung

One day when we were young
One wonderful morning in May
You told me you loved me
When we were young one day*

That was sixty years ago, in a seaside city. Today I'm visiting him in the locked ward of a nursing home inland. He does not seem to remember the between years, with his two wives, my three husbands.

Calling me by the intimate old name, he holds out his hand and says, quite clearly: 'Let's get a milkshake before we go to the party. I'll buy you a double if you can drink it.'

Then the lids shut over his teenage eyes and he drifts away again.

> *when none remain*
> *who remember things,*
> *does that mean*
> *they never happened –*
> *foam ebbs with the tide*

* This is the first verse of an old song with music by Johann Strauss and lyrics by Oscar Hammerstein II. The second verse begins 'Sweet songs of youth were sung'.

published in *Ribbons*, USA

Pink On Green On White

I'd never thought of gardening as a competitive sport. If it is, I certainly don't have the knowledge, or the zeal, to take part.

Nonetheless, my rather spindly young crèpe myrtle tree is now flourishing a cluster of blooms against the white back wall of the house, while my envious friend's trees are not even in bud.

> *with my smartphone*
> *I photograph the result*
> *of laissez-faire*
> *in my courtyard, deep pink*
> *above glossy green leaves*

published in *The Moorings*, Australia

And a Happy New Year!

Old-style Christmas cards, with greetings and sometimes brief letters, put in envelopes and posted. Every year I receive and send out fewer. Partly because at the age I am, a number of my relatives and friends have died or drifted away. Partly because some of those remaining have espoused the technology of e-cards, prefer to text their good wishes, or to telephone for a chat.

I treasure the cards that I do receive from family and friends not seen during the year, especially if they include update messages. But mostly such letters contain details of their grandchildren's accomplishments, with perhaps a mention of their own medical problems. Little of the nitty gritty of their lives is revealed.

> *how do I feel*
> *how do they feel, facing*
> *shortened futures?*
> *talk of the here and now*
> *overlays deeper thoughts*

published in *Kokako*, NZ

Not All Frogs Turn Into Princes

Across the road from the cinema, we find a French crêperie, the Four Frogs.

My granddaughter chooses a chocolate confection for her supper, while I indulge in nostalgia. The last time Grand Marnier flambéed my dessert was almost fifty years ago.
And I was with a man I might have married.

> *more memorable*
> *than the lovemaking,*
> *those crêpes suzettes*
> *with which he wooed me –*
> *à la Recherche*…*

* Reference to 'the episode of the madeleine' in volume I of Marcel Proust's 1913 *A la Recherche du Temps Perdu*, translated as *Remembrance of Times Past*.

published in *CHO, Contemporary Haibun Online*

And Yet, This Choice

the tedium
of household shopping...
list ticked off
I'm floating my thoughts
beyond this supermarket

'How are you today?' asks the middle-aged checkout chick mechanically.
'I'm fine, How are you?' I respond.

'I'm just wondering if my dog will still be alive when I get home after this shift.'
Picking up my packet of turkey mince, she bursts into tears.

The queue behind me hastily moves to another counter, while I listen. I learn that she has a rescue pooch Orlando who is now old and infirm. He was moving around when she had to leave for work, but seemed very weak.

'Um, the vet?' I suggest.
'No, if I take him to the vet, they'll only want to put him down. I rescued him. I can't put my boy to sleep, not yet.'

All I can do is whisper, 'You'll know when the time is right,' and give her a hug.

Neither of us says have a great day.

> *we can do*
> *for our beloved pets*
> *what we cannot*
> *for our people*
> *and yet, this choice...*

published in *CHO, Contemporary Haibun Online*

Summers to Remember

2016 an ambulance takes him from our home forever
2017 his mind has died, his body is dying
2018 the cancer monster ravages my daughter's beloved
2019 our country and its wild life destroyed by bushfires
2020 a new pandemic strikes

Too much tragedy... Is it because I am old now?

> *childhood summers*
> *day after day the beach*
> *with family –*
> *the worst that happened then,*
> *sunburn or rained-out picnics*

Bucket List

swimming through
a sickly childhood
by the sea
books, classical music,
always care from family

Mozart's clarinet concerto in A major soars above the veldt in *Out of Africa*. Fills the living room with joy whenever my grandson practices for his audition.

My bucket half full, I would love to visit Salzburg. And I would love to hear Stephen play again in the Seattle Symphony Orchestra.

Time enough later, perhaps… Right now, I am putting a $1,000 deposit on my dream of touring the Moorish sites of southern Spain.

a longish life
rich in experience,
in many loves…
greedy to desire more
yet, I do, oh I do

'Days May Not Be Fair, Always...'*

a small home
a small family
an abundance
of loving, good cooking
and sounds of the sea

'Always' was their song, As a child, I heard it often, sung in Grandma's rich voice while she did the housework.

At balls and wedding receptions we attended en famille, my grandfather, Pop, inevitably requested the band play Always. He would take Grandma in his arms, and with eyes only for each other, they would waltz around and around.

Pop survived Gallipoli, then stayed in work during the Great Depression. Their only son fought in Papua New Guinea. A granddaughter almost died in the polio epidemic. Money was tight.

Their fiftieth wedding anniversary celebrated in style. Dapper in his tuxedo, Pop stood, holding silver-haired Grandma tightly to his side, and made a short speech thanking her and all the family for his happiness.

She kissed him; then gazing at her Eddie, sang in a still strong soprano the opening bars, *I'll be loving you, always*, continuing word perfect to the end.

> *I listen now*
> *to Kiri Te Kanawa,*
> *her 'Always'*
> *no more beautiful than*
> *Grandma who lived her love*

* The song 'Always' was composed by Irving Berlin in 1925, and has been recorded by many artists, including Billie Holiday, Frank Sinatra, Paul McCartney, and Kiri Te Kanawa. The original music is in waltz time.

published in *Kokako*, NZ

Out of the Blue

March festival
hot-air balloons drifting
through the morning...
'how colourful', we say
'what fun to be aloft'

I'm standing at the corner of the parkland, chatting with a fellow dog-walker. Suddenly a black Labrador comes racing up the middle of the road. Spooked, I'm sure, by the sight and sounds of huge bright balloons so low overhead.

No owner. No lead. No way to halt its frantic flight.

running
away from terror
running
towards the junction
and...please, no

A Tall Window

seeking neither
the moon nor the stars,
I'm happiest
in the hours of sunlight
the mornings of birdsong

I greet the days. Fill them with music, friends, activities.

Shadows shift on my white courtyard walls. Late afternoons, low on physical energy. I loll in a blue velvet recliner. Reading…musing.

swinging, nibbling
through the ash tree branches
five king parrots
flash vermillion breasts –
the world from my window

published in *Drifting Sands*, online

Giving

My grandson texts me from America, that he has something for me. He's not an ungenerous boy, but too young for a part-time job, has no funds with which to buy gifts.

So...today he facetimes, seated at the piano in the Seattle family home where they are currently 'sheltering in place', (as it's called over there), from covid-19 and plays the first two movements of Beethoven's Moonlight Sonata without hesitation. I didn't even know he had learned that beautiful piece yet.

Then he looks up, smiling at me.

> *the miracles*
> *of modern technology*
> *the miracles*
> *of love and music flowing*
> *through generations.*

published in *International Tanka*, Japan

Where Have All the Tulips Gone*

white tulips…
a formal wedding
blushing bride
sheathed in white satin,
virgin for this day

Though tulips are glorious in the fields, they are not my favourite cut flowers. I prefer strongly scented blooms.

Of course my husband would have known that, had he cared to put it into his memory. The day after our first daughter was born, he brought a great bunch of tulips to the hospital. Beautiful yellow tulips which certainly brightened the institutional ambience. But they did that tulip thing, hanging their heads from the vase. And they gave no scent.

April Violets
my favourite perfume,
finished –
thorns on the red roses
of romantic love

After his dutiful visit, as I lay in bed hurting all over, an old song was humming through my head. 'When it's spring again, I'll bring again, tulips from Amsterdam…'†

Neither of us had been to Amsterdam, but a high school class-mate, Margaret, and I were taken with that song. We used to annoy our friends by performing it at lunchtimes in the school grounds. Margaret had thick, wavy, hair the colour of flaming tulip petals.

Six months after the birth of my daughter, I was home from Tokyo visiting my family. One morning I wheeled Emiko in a pram to the local shops, where I met by chance Margaret's mother. I was shocked to learn Margaret had recently died.

> *rock-a-bye*
> *my precious baby,*
> *rest in peace*
> *my funny red-haired friend*
> *our seasons turn, turn...*

For many years after her death, conflating Margaret and our flower song, I couldn't bear tulips.

Then one fine day in 1988 when we were living in Canberra, I took my daughters to the first Floriade spring flower festival. Impossible not to admire the beds and beds of tulips in every hue and shape, blooming throughout Commonwealth Park.

At some stage, a ferris wheel was added to this annual celebration. Over the years my favourite thing was to ride it and survey the colours of spring, and Floriade's patterns, from above.

> *ferris wheel*
> *go round and round again!*
> *memories*
> *last a day for you,*
> *a lifetime for me‡*

Now we are approaching spring 2020. A global pandemic has cancelled planning for Floriade in the park, after thirty-three years. Instead, in an effort to raise our spirits, there is to be 'Floriade Reimagined', an adapted format of the festival with, they say, over a million bulbs and annuals flowering across the city.

> *in the face*
> *of worldwide tragedy,*
> *how trivial*
> *the absence of massed tulips*
> *and yet, and yet…*

* 'Where Have All the Flowers Gone', Peter Seeger

† 'Tulips from Amsterdam', originally written in German. A hit version in English, sung by Max Bygraves, was number 3 on the UK pop chart in 1958.

‡ Original Japanese tanka by the contemporary poet, Kuriki Kyoko, translated by Amelia.

'We'll Meet Again…'

Except we might not.
Dame Vera Lynn has died at the age of 103.
Her simple, optimistic, songs with catchy tunes made Lynn the
sweetheart of wartime Britain, a voice of resilience in the 1940s.

Recently, in response to the covid-19 pandemic, Queen Eliza-
beth II made a speech to her nation, which reverberated around
the English-speaking world, quoting from one of Lynn's best
loved numbers, '… We'll meet again, Don't know where, Don't
know when, But I know we'll meet again some sunny day.'

> *a single death*
> *among hundreds of thousands*
> *across the globe…*
> *yet I remember her song,*
> *remember those stories*

During eight weeks of lockdown, that anthem of hope often
played in my head. Cocooned with a four-legged companion,
isolated from family and friends, I needed its comfort.

> *this is home*
> *full of family photos*
> *this is home*
> *where a white dog lives*
> *with our memories*

Now when socialising has cautiously resumed, my local friends
and I are meeting once more.

I think, though, of the many nice, interesting people I have known over a rich lifetime of almost eighty years. People whom I am unlikely to see again. Some of them – sadly, quite a large number – I am aware are no longer alive. With others, in Australia, Japan, England, Morocco, Malta, North America, I've lost contact.

Sometimes a former friend comes to mind, appearing as she or he was when we were close. And I ponder whether that friend ever thinks of me with the same appreciation for what we once shared, or with the same regret that life intervened to drift us apart.

> *wondering*
> *if and how and where*
> *they are living –*
> *newly-planted lavender*
> *flourishes in my garden*

Voices Fading

Amelia Fielden (A) and Jan Foster (J)

> *through the drizzle*
> *a rainbow of feathers*
> *eastern rosellas*
> *arcing over the park –*
> *one moment at a time*   A

Approaching the hospital for an appointment with my specialist, my mind is jangling with the news of yet more deaths recorded overnight from this awful virus engulfing our nation. But as the automatic doors slide open, I step into what seems an alternate universe. The air is filled with a silver shower of harp music, notes fall free and soothing as summer rain. The harpist is seated by the glass front wall, a halo of sunlight around her adding to the illusion of unreality. I breathe deeply, my spirit already lighter than moments before.

> *peaceful drift*
> *of lotus flowers*
> *afloat*
> *over the surface*
> *of the murky depths*   J

The last time I visited Nara…with overseas travel now banned due to a pandemic, perhaps the final time…was only three months after knee surgery. I hobble along gravel paths to the pond spread wide in front of Tōdaiji temple. Sharing a welcome bench with a teenager in school uniform, I wait.

> *willow fronds*
> *dipping in green shallows…*
> *you arrive*
> *with an apology*
> *as always too late*　　　　　A

In response to an invitation from my artist friend, I've come to the gallery which is hosting an exhibition of her work. Not a fan of her particular style, which is too abstract for my taste, I am already regretting my gesture of support. What will I find to say to those inside, and how quickly can I make my escape? Yet, as I navigate my way through shoals of aficionados, it is easy to sail along on a raft of social platitudes.

> *voices fading*
> *behind me in the night air*
> *a soft breeze*
> *sends clouds wafting*
> *across the face of the moon*　　　J

published in *CHO, Contemporary Haibun Online*

E Lucevan Le Stelle*

You speak to me now of you and your no longer mortal beloved, as twin stars in the Southern Cross.

Almost half a century ago, the stars hung bright over the Mediterranean as we sailed through the night from Catania to Valletta. A crescent moon on the sky's velvet, salted humid air, the rocking of gentle black waves…more beguiling than the ferry saloon.

So I sat up on the deck, your small body shawled to my heart. And wished that I could keep you safe and free from sorrow, always.

> *there are limits*
> *to a mother's powers,*
> *no limits*
> *to a mother's love…*
> *that hard bench, your soft body*

* 'And the Stars Look Down', the title of an aria in Puccini's opera *Tosca*

Unspoken Eulogy

my father
grew dahlias and sweet peas
wept hearing
Beethoven's 'Ode to Joy',
read books all his spare time

A wartime child, I never had a teddy bear. My earliest play-thing, a stuffed white dog, was called Pongo by my father. After that he bought me a real puppy, And books, lots of books.

my father
home from his city office,
jacket pocket
bulky with childrens' stories
from second-hand bookshops

He taught me that libraries were where the wider world could be found. A penny lending library in our little beachside shopping street. The Mitchell Library at the end of Sunday tram rides with Daddy.

my father
setting out on Saturdays
with a string bag
full of books to return
and his ink-darkened library card

In the small case we brought home from his final hospital stay were a change of pyjamas and an Ian Rankin novel.

published in *Ribbons*, USA

'Play it Sam'

      Casablanca last century.
Bogart and Bergmann yearning at Rick's American Café, in the early 40s.
A diplomat and his young wife partying at the Hotel Atlantique, in the early 70s.
      Different worlds.
More remote than ever now, with borders closed by a pandemic.
Still, the fundamental things apply.

> *as time goes by*
> and winter frosts my mind,
> *no matter*
> *what the future brings*
> *I must remember this*
>
> *moonlight and love songs…*

Expressions in italics are taken from the lyrics of the song 'As Time Goes By', written by Hermann Hupfeld in 1931.

Terminus

On a blustery midday soon after trams start running, a flock of grandmothers, from Canberra High 'class of '58', gathers at Civic for a joy ride to Gungahlin.

Settling into a vermillion carriage, I look around at familiar faces: 3 called Robyn; 7 who sat in the same classrooms from the age of nine; 15 who went through high school together; 8 of us now widows. I can't count the schoolmates we have lost.

Terminus reached, we crowd a nearby Chinese restaurant. Chatting and eating. Eating and chatting. Jasmine tea and a queue for the Ladies.

The end of the line. But not quite yet. After lunch, we tram back to the city to resume separate lives. For how long, I wonder.

> *we reminisce*
> *about our shared pasts,*
> *talk a lot*
> *of present times, but*
> *little of the future*

Wild Lives

Fourteen years at the coast house. Lots of visitors. One morning there was a lizard lolling on top of the backyard solar water tank. Seemingly unafraid, it accepted scraps of fruit and vegetables placed near its mouth. 'An Eastern water dragon,' explained my son-in-law, the invited guest.

The dragon stayed for a few weeks. Then suddenly it was nowhere to be seen.

My adolescent grandson's favourite word at the time was 'random'.

> *spring after spring*
> *wild yellow daisy weeds,*
> *mown down again...*
> *this life of appearances*
> *and disappearances*

published in *CHO, Contemporary Haibun Online*

Hark the Herald Angels Sing

late afternoon
such anticipation
on Christmas Eve
warm kitchen aromas
rustle of gift wrapping

My back to the French windows, I'm playing a leisurely game of Monopoly with my grandson.
He jumps up. 'It's snowing, look!'

Three years later, we are separated by the Pacific Ocean and a raging pandemic. Stephen texts me a photo I don't recall him taking. There I am on the back deck in Seattle, pine-green sweater starred with snowflakes, palms upturned to catch my first white Christmas.

azure sky
this summer December
listening alone
to radio carols
waiting for family facetime

published in *Kokako*, NZ

Responsive Tanka Strings

Creating Sunshine

Jan Foster and *Amelia Fielden*

each breath
like shards of broken glass
this morning
out walking I count down
the number of days to spring

twin trees
of palest pink blossom
trunks encircled
with white daffodils –
crying from a double pram

outside my window
an act of urban terrorism –
a mob
of marauding sparrows
on the newly seeded lawn

'summertime
and the living is easy'
swimming along
amused by teenage grand kids –
seize the day oh seize the day

a small girl
in rain hat and rubber boots
splashes joyously
creating her own sunshine
– that's what puddles are meant for

published in *Kokako*, NZ

Perspectives

Amelia Fielden and *Jan Foster*

engagement photo
at Lake Yamanaka
the mountain
rising snow-streaked behind,
in the foreground just us

cool undertones
to your smiling comments
I search your eyes
…it's dangerous
to love someone this much

fearlessly
my granddaughter plunges
under the waves –
loving and letting go,
an eternal quandary

hanging baskets
a waterfall of blossoms
tumbling
around me, clouds of perfume
…I'm free to dream

Je Reviens
always my favourite
French perfume
remembered by one lover
…only by him

adrift on a raft
of social platitudes
I detect
a whiff of ozone
ahead of the coming storm

swept away
by a 'southerly buster'
the suspicion
I should be somewhere else
doing something useful

clearing pathways
through the storm's debris
it's alarming
how good at this
our family has become

surrounded
in old age by family,
not my karma –
though love can bridge distance
one plus none is still one

across the abyss
of loneliness, a lifeline
…this new friend
who shares my passion
for travelling

'better
to travel hopefully
than to arrive' –
hope is the blessing,
regard these late blooms!

flights cancelled
long delays announced –
time
to rethink
the way ahead

Celebrations

Jan Foster and *Amelia Fielden*

climbing rose
scratches at the window
seeking attention
the cat winds herself
around my ankles

this quiet year
no new health issues –
I invest
in gold rose bushes
for my bare garden bed

footsteps on my roof
this early Christmas night
…sadly not Santa
but possums on the prowl
heading for my vegie patch

feeling sorry
for the stuffed turkey
I heap my plate
with roasted potatoes:
December dinner with Dad

alone
this summer solstice night
I celebrate
wind, water, starlit skies
 – Australia's southern coast

all that water
in the rolling ocean,
none falling
from drought-dusty skies…
ever a wide brown land

party quests
enjoying the season
at the beach
Southern Right whale and her calf
blow festive spouts off shore

gulls in the blue
dipping and rising
above wave crests –
come with me to the sea
while our tide is still high

Moorings

Amelia Fielden and *Jan Foster*

line of sight:
deep blue lake, white sailboat
spruce forest
mountain peaks, unclouded sky –
just this, for now

subtle warmth
of treasure spread out
on the pages
so much of value said
in so few words

one daughter
only phones or emails me,
the other
goes with pen, paper, and stamp –
time flows on, love is constant

at uni
I faced piles of paperwork
today
my granddaughter
does it all online

years and years
of busy family life
followed
by Facebook, and a dog
in silence at my feet

alone again
I slip my moorings
setting off
to find the way
back to myself

published in *Ribbons*, USA

Sweetness Harvested

Amelia Fielden and *Jan Foster*

no breath of breeze
yet the golden ash leaves
dance as they fall –
at ninety-six my aunt
now steering a wheelchair

pruning shrubs
of their spent season's blooms,
it's time
for my next cut and colour
…maybe even a manicure

gentle and strong
those beloved hands…I wear
his wedding ring
removed before cremation –
garden fires forbidden here

yellow moon
riding in a smoke-filled sky
cane stubble burning –
sweetness harvested
ahead of the coming cold

first frost
whitens the mulching piles
next weekend
a pumpkin festival,
'if winter comes …'*

* From 'Ode to the West Wind' by Percy Bysshe Shelley
published in *Ribbons*, USA

In Every Season

Amelia Fielden and *Jan Foster*

grandpa group
at the local coffee shop
not much talking
just the ease of old mates
now retired from battle

gunshots, screams,
running footsteps,
sirens,
…urban street music
set to strobing lights

Rigoletto
contemporary style
so relevant
to Trump's America
but oh, the singing

my journey
through the rainforest
set to music
courtesy of nature
…bellbirds

travelling on
conscious of how rich
my life has been
in every season
I hear the mourning doves

published in *Ribbons*, USA

Two's a crowd

Amelia Fielden and *Jan Foster*

Tuesday morning …
my fortnightly cleaner
Ana's coming
an event in the long months
of slow-paced senior life

in this time of plague
self-isolation they say
a necessity
to stay well and whole –
I love my solitude

no TV
in the 'olden days'
when Gran played
a card game called Patience –
my dog can't chat with me

drawn outside
by a raucous gathering
I eavesdrop
on excited twittering
from the bird bath

two's a crowd
according to current rules
on distancing
for all those who are
neither furred nor feathered

on a remote beach
your beard brushes my chin
seagulls
the only witnesses
to our illicit embrace

published in *Kokako*, NZ

Days of Our Lives

Amelia Fielden and *Genie Nakano*

the glossiness
of magpies on dewy grass –
morning walk
with today's plans settled,
small dog on her leash, smiling

moistened earth
drought finally over –
tomorrow
two doctor's appointments,
I keep feeling spring

time to shop
fresh fruits at the market
all healthy stuff
to push back my ageing –
face-timing the grandkids

a nurse tells me
'I can't believe your age' –
blushing pink
my hip replacement
bequeaths a new life

al fresco lunch
old school friends fifty years on
still full of life
crepe myrtle blooming crimson
in the warm blue air

salsa, cumbia
meringue those hips –
my new love
teaching zumba to seniors
'si como no' yes why not

violet dusk
drifts through the eucalypts –
desk lamp lit
I ponder a manuscript
of Japanese tanka

too tired to cook
so tonight our favourite
Izakaya
for high mountain vegies
shochu and fresh oysters

dinner for one
the latest bestseller
propped by my plate,
blinds open to glimpses
of the Southern Cross stars

nightime
together in a queen bed
two senior dogs
hubby and I float away
in a symphony of snores

slow dark hours
dreaming of what has been –
in the morning
must text my daughter
to say I'm still alive

published in *Atlas Poetica*, USA

Uncovering

Carmel Summers and *Amelia Fielden*

I prepare
a goose-feather doona
for my winter bed
the first tips of jonquils
emerge from cover outside

in April
the earth remains warm enough
to plant saplings –
grevillea roots spread
in the hole for his ashes

an excavation
that became our capital's lake…
rowers cut Vs
that sparkle brighter
than diamonds

old movies
old prejudices –
shocked now
by the incorrectness
of Breakfast at Tiffany's

woken too early
by squabbling mynahs
and a hungry cat
learning to adapt
in an ever-changing world

just when I thought
this year would be better,
came the news
of his diagnosis –
autumn leaves in rare rain

if we could predict
our fate with each dawn
would we arise –
the deeper the shadows
the brighter the sun

the colours
of Impressionism
so vibrant,
yet it is Monet's snowscape
lingering behind my eyes

splashes of colour
in her opal pendant
unlucky, they say…
opportunities we miss
under the sway of others

why ever
did I let myself
be dissuaded
from those teenage dreams –
parents have such power

a currawong lurks
near the rosella's nest
nature is not kind –
a hierarchy of needs
yet still this drive to write

the bald eagle
snatches up a squirrel –
how to explain
survival of the fittest
to my watching grandchild

a hawk's shadow
drifts across the lake
in silence –
some are quiet achievers
others crave acclaim

turned seventy
my cousin is training
for the UK
Veterans' rowing comp –
fog blurs the morning river

hardly visible
in a clinging strand of mist
my neighbour's house
yet the discord of their words
cannot be hidden

'love thy neighbour'
a compassionate adage
but my neighbour
is a rose-eating possum –
should I plant cacti?

flitting through the weeds
in my overgrown garden
six fairy wrens
on this chill Canberra day
my footsteps become lighter

Many Shades

Amelia Fielden and *Genie Nakano*

in old age
mirroring childhood
my desires shrink
to a room wih a view
of surf breaking on the sand

the footprints
of a child, sandcastle
left behind
I add some driftwood
to a tidal canvas

those Sundays
exploring galleries
Dad and I
no talent ourselves,
just a love of paintings

as we walk
in the rose garden
butterflies
dancing to birdsong...
the soft sound of wings

many shades
of flowers, of pencils
assembled
for my return to colouring
pictures in a covid book

in my journal
a broad spectrum of blooms
pressed between
poems and jottings
from solitary days

About the Author

Amelia Fielden was born in Sydney, Australia, in December 1941. She is an internationally awarded translator and poet.

Qualifications

Bachelor of Asian Studies (Japanese Honours) Australian National University, Canberra; Graduate Diploma of Teaching, Secondary Education, University of Adelaide, South Australia.

Graduate Diploma of Translation (Japanese) University of Canberra.

Master of Arts (Japanese Literature) University of Newcastle, New South Wales;

Masters' Thesis: *An Annotated Translation of My Tanka Diary* by KawanoYūko

Career

1965–2003 researcher, teacher, translator

Since retiring from full-time work as a senior translator of Japanese for the Australian government in Canberra, Amelia has specialised in translating Japanese literature – primarily, but not exclusively, tanka poetry.

Books Translated or Co-translated by Amelia

On Tsukuba Peak: 2000 tanka collection by Kawamura Hatsue; bilingual; Wollongong, NSW, Five Islands Press, 2002

Time Passes (Saigetsu): 1995 tanka collection by Kawano Yūko; bilingual; Canberra, ACT, Ginninderra Press, 2002

Vital Forces (Tairyoku): 1998 tanka collection by Kawano Yūko; bilingual; co-translated with Yuhki Aya; Nagoya, Japan, Bookpark, 2004

Behind Summer (Natsu no Ushiro): 2003 tanka collection by Kuriki Kyōko; co-translated with Yuhki Aya; Canberra, ACT, Ginninderra Press, 2005

As Things Are: 100 tanka selected by Manaka Tomohisa from 10 collections by Kawano Yūko; Canberra, ACT, Ginninderra Press, 2005

On This Same Star ('Will'): 2003 tanka collection by Kitakubo Mariko; bilingual; Tokyo Japan, Kadokawa Shoten, 2006

My Tanka Diary (Hizuke no Aru Uta): 2002 tanka poetry diary with prose commentaries by Kawano Yūko; Canberra, ACT, Ginninderra Press, 2006

Ferris Wheel: 101 Modern and Contemporary Japanese Tanka, the work of 56 Japanese poets; co-translated with Kozue Uzawa, bilingual, Boston, USA, Cheng and T'sui, 2006

Awarded the 2007 prize for translation of Japanese Literature by Columbia University, New York, USA; also known as the Donald Keene award.*

Raffaello's Azure: tanka poetry and essays by Hazama Ruri; co-translated with the author; bilingual; Tokyo, Japan, Tanka Kenkyusha 2006

Cicada Forest: anthology of the work of Kitakubo Mariko; bilingual; Tokyo, Japan; Kadokawa Shoten, 2008

Kaleidoscope: selected tanka of Terayama Shuji; co-translated with Uzawa Kozue; bilingual; Tokyo, Japan Hokuseidō, 2008

Doorway to the Sky (Sora no Tobira): tanka collection by Tanaka Noriko; co-translated with Ogi Saeko; bilingual; Tokyo, Japan, Tanka Kenkyusha, 2008

Aster Flower (Shion): 2009 tanka collection by Kusumi Fusako; bilingual with colour plates; Tenri City, Japan, Tenrijihōsha, 2009

The Time of This World: 100 tanka selected by Ōshima Shiyō from 13 collections by Kawano Yūko; Baltimore, Maryland, USA, Modern English Tanka Press, 2010

Breast Clouds (Nyubōin): award-winning 2008 tanka collection by Tanaka Noriko; co-translated with Ogi Saeko; bilingual; Tokyo, Japan, Tanka Kenkyusha, 2010

Snow Crystal Star-shaped: anthology of tanka poetry by Konno Mari; bilingual, Tokyo, Japan, Kadokawa Shoten, 2010

The Maternal Line (Bōkei): 2008 tanka collection by Kawano Yūko; co-translated with Ogi Saeko; Baltimore, Maryland, USA, Modern English Tanka Press, 2011

A bluish White Light 'a cry from the heart'; tanka about the Fukushima Nuclear Power Plant, by Satō Yūtei; edited by Yasunaga Tatsumi; Matsudo, Japan, JARC Corporation, 2013 (available on amazon, com in paperback or as Amazon 2014 Kindle edition)

Tanka to Eat: themed tanka masterpieces by modern and contemporary Japanese poets, selected and presented with commentaries by Tanaka Noriko; co-translated with Ogi Saeko; bilingual; Port Adelaide, South Australia, Ginninderra Press, 2014

From the Middle country (Naka no Kuni Yori); 2013 collection by Tanaka Noriko; co-translated with Ogi Saeko; Port Adelaide, South Australia, Ginninderra Press, 2015

The Journey of My Life: tanka composed by May Yen Ting translated by Amelia Fielden, with commentaries and prose translated by Steven Ting; edited by Link-Erl Ting and Warren Wu; USA, Amazon Prime Paperback, 2014

Lovely Kimono: themed haiku and tanka by modern and contemporary Japanese poets, selected and presented with commentaries by Tanaka Noriko; co-translated with Ogi Saeko; Port Adelaide, South Australia, Ginninderra Press, 2016

For Instance, Sweetheart (Tatoeba Kimi): Forty Years of Love Songs; autobiographical essays and tanka poems written to each other by Kawano Yūko and her husband, Nagata Kazuhiro; first published in Japanese by Bungei Shunshu Tokyo, in 2011; Amelia Fielden, translated edition, Port Adelaide, South Australia Ginninderra Press, 2017

Four Poets in a Boat: An Anthology of Contemporary Japanese Tanka; selected by Ogi Saeko; co-translated with Ogi Saeko; Port Adelaide, South Australia, Ginninderra Press, 2018

Poetry Bridges: Canberra/Nara Commemorative Anthology; edited and co-translated with Ogi Saeko and Tanaka Noriko; bilingual; Port Adelaide, South Australia, Ginninderra Press, 2018

Destiny (Unmei): a collection of Japanese tanka by May Yen Ting translated by Amelia Fielden; edited by Ling-Erl Ting and Warren Wu; bilingual; USA, Quadu Press, 2019

Two Countries (Kuni Futatsu): a collection of Japanese tanka by May Yen Ting translated by Amelia Fielden; edited by Ling-Erl Ting and Warren Wu; bilingual, USA Quadu Press 2019

Lily of the Valley: 2018/2019 tanka collection by Kusumi Fusako; bilingual with colourplates; Tenri City, Japan, Tenrijihōsha, 2020

Original Poetry and Prose written in English by Amelia Fielden

Eucalypt and Iris Streams: poetry about Australia and Japan in various forms; bilingual, Japanese translations by Ogi Saeko; Canberra, ACT, Ginninderra Press 2001

Fountains Play and Time Passes: original tanka in English by Amelia Fielden, together with her translations of selections from *Time Passes* (Saigetsu) by Kawano Yūko; bilingual, Japanese translations of Amelia's tanka by Ogi Saeko; Canberra, ACT, Ginninderra Press, 2002

Short Songs: individual tanka poems and multi-tanka sequences; Canberra, ACT, Ginninderra Press, 2002

Still Swimming: individual tanka poems, plus multi-sequences and strings; Canberra, ACT, Ginninderra Press, 2005

Baubles, Bangles & Beads: Threaded Tanka; Canberra, ACT, Ginninderra Press, 2007

Light on Water: a collection of individual tanka, sequences and strings published between 2006 and 2010 in international journals and anthologies; Port Adelaide, South Australia, Ginninderra Press, 2010

Mint Tea From a Copper Pot & Other Tanka Tales: some stories of my life, in poetry and prose; Port Adelaide, South Australia, Ginninderra Press, 2013

These Purple Years: a collection of individual tanka, sequences and strings, and tanka tales published between 2011 and 2017, in international journals and anthologies; Port Adelaide, South Australia, Ginninderra Press, 2018

Collaborations with Other Poets

In Two Minds: responsive tanka in themed chapters, written with Australian poet, Kathy Kituai; Baltimore, Maryland, USA, Modern English Tanka Press, 2008

Weaver Birds: a bilingual responsive tanka diary written and translated with Japanese-Australian poet, Saeko Ogi; bilingual; Port Adelaide, South Australia, Ginninderra Press, 2010

Yesterday, Today and Tomorrow: a calendar year of responsibe tanka written with Australian poet, Kathy Kituai; Brisbane, Queensland, Interactive Press, 2011

Words Flower From One to Another: responsive tanka in themed chapters written with Japanese-Australian poet Saeko Ogi; bilingual; Brisbane, Queensland, Interactive Press, 2011

Conversations in Tanka between Amelia Fielden, Jan Foster, and Friends; several different forms of responsive tanka writing, composed by 23 poets from Australia, France, Japan, New Zealand, South Africa and USA; Port Adelaide, South Australia, Ginninderra Press, 2014

Colouring in: the Four Seasons of Four Poets: Amelia Fielden, Gerry Jacobson, Genie Nakano and Neal Whitman writing, in Australia-American pairs, responsive tanka strings on spring, summer, autumn, and winter; Port Adelaide, South Australia Ginninderra Press, 2016

Tanks Anthologies Edited or Co-edited

Food For Thought: an anthology of new tanka on a theme, written by 45 Australians, collected and edited; Port Adelaide, South Australia, Ginninderra Press, 2011

The Melody Lingers On: an anthology of tanka on musical themes, written by 55 Australian poets, collected and edited; Port Adelaide, South Australia, Ginninderra Press, 2012

100 Tanka by 100 Poets of Australia and New Zealand – one poem each: selected and edited by Amelia Fielden, Beverley George and Patricia Prime; Port Adelaide, South Australia, Ginninderra Press, 2013

Storyteller: individual tanka, tanka sequences (some written responsively with other poets) and tanka prose by Genie Nakano (USA), edited by Amelia Fielden and Ellen Weston; California, USA, Purple Aura Press, 2014

All You Need Is Love: tanka on the theme of 'love' interpreted broadly by 62 Australian poets; Port Adelaide, South Australia, Ginninderra Press, 2015

Poems to Wear: a Japan/Australian production; Part I; Japanese tanka selected, with added commentaries, by Noriko Tanaka, and translated by Amelia Fielden and Saeko Ogi; Part II Australian tanka collected and edited by Amelia

Fielden; Port Adelaide, South Australia, Ginninderra Press, 2016

Poetry Bridges: Canberra/Nara Commemorative Anthology; collected, edited, and translated with Ogi Saeko and Tanaka Noriko; bilingual; Port Adelaide, South Australia, Ginninderra Press, 2018

(All of the above books published since 2013 by Ginninderra Press are still available for purchase at www.ginninderrapress. com.au)

Poetry-related Activities

Member of the Japan Tanka Poets' Society since 1999

Member of the Tanka Society of America since 2000

Foundation Member of the Limestone Tanka Poets, Canberra, Australia

Member of the following Canberra poetry workshopping groups: Majura Café Poets, Moorings, The Poem Nest, Tram Stop Poets, Lyrebird Tanka Circle; and the Wollongong groups Poetry in the City and Poetry Circles.

English tanka and tanka tales published regularly in journals worldwide – for example in *Eucalypt* (Australia); *International Tanka* (Japan); *Kokako* (New Zealand); *Skylark* (UK), *Atlas Poetica, red lights, Ribbons* (USA); *Cattails, CHO, Haibun Today, Drifting Sands* (online); and in several international anthologies.

Presenter of translation seminars and tanka workshops in Australia, Canada, Japan and USA

Participated in International Tanka Conventions in 2000 (Vancouver), 2006 (Honolulu), 2009 (Tokyo). In 2009 was one of the judges of the associated English tanka competition.

Appeared on NHK television programs with Kawano Yūko in 2000 and 2005.

Foreign guest representative at the Imperial Palace, Tokyo, for the Annual Imperial New Year Poetry Gathering, in January 2008.

Other Interests

Travel, Japan, swimming, reading, language studies, attending ballet and opera performances, enjoying the company of family, friends and pets.

Printed in Australia
AUHW022038071221
356676AU00004B/5